EVER-CHANGING PERSPECTIVES

A Simple Book
for a Complex Life

GW00480611

GARETH MICHAEL

Visit www.garethmichael.com to read more about the author.

You will also find author events, and you can sign up for e-newsletters so that you're always the first to hear about new releases.

ISBN: 978-1-79-791038-3

Dedication

To My Big Sister and Angel,
Lisa-Marie

If it wasn't for the gift and loss of your pure life,
I would never have been able to experience mine.

This book is for you.

♡

Contents

Introduction

I f you were to ask me why I wrote this book, I'd say I wrote it to try to assist others. But, as it turned out, I was writing it for the person who needed it the most—me. I didn't understand how much I needed it until it was in front of me and, unknown to me at the time, how it would help guide me through the very challenging year that lay ahead.

I struggled to reason why this book—or, indeed, why any of my writings or quotes—should be shared with anyone other than myself, especially since I've struggled to understand my own thoughts and emotions for as long as I can remember. I'm dyslexic (I spelled dyslexic wrong, again, even while writing this), so writing this book was a struggle for me. I had no plan, no visible structure, a lot of emotion, and many unknown, unwritten parts with little to no direction as to how to move ahead. That sounds quite similar to the life that lies ahead for many of us now.

At the beginning of 2019—after countless nights of sitting up until 3 am writing and a lot of hands-on support with editing—all 20 writings contained in this book were complete. I feel these writings came out of me at a time when I was mentally and emotionally strong—a part of me, somewhere deep down, must have known what was going to be in store over the following months, when I felt quite the opposite.

Throughout that difficult time, the messaging in each writing seemed to be ever-changing from one reading to the next, depending on where I was mentally or emotionally on the day when I decided to pick up the book. These writings helped me to feel when I was incapable of feeling, they gave me answers when I had only questions, and they also gave me questions to think about that brought answers from myself I didn't know I needed. They gave me a different perspective on other people's lives that allowed me to gain a greater understanding of my own.

This book is now finally being released—a full year after it was completed. I decided not to release this book when I finished it, but I couldn't understand why at the time. It turns out I had to do my own journey with it before I could share it with others so it could become a part of theirs. Whether you love it or hate it, agree or disagree with it, I'd like you to be honest with yourself about what you truly think and feel about it. Honestly, this is all that matters!

This is the first and last you'll hear from me. The writings that lie ahead are all about you and your journey. That journey can only have a start, a middle, and an end with you guiding the way. So, it's in your hands from here!

Wishing you love & support from my journey to yours.
Gareth Michael

How to Use this Book

The title of the book represents how your perspective on things is ever-changing, even regarding your own life, relationships, friendships, career, body. It's worth remembering that your own perspective is ever-changing, and so your perspective on this book will evolve depending on where you are in your life.

There's no right or wrong way to read or use this book. Many people read a writing a day or one a week, allowing themselves the time to process each one. The writings are direct, concentrated, straight to the point. It can be a good idea to take your time and allow yourself the space to think deeply upon each writing and what it means to you.

After each writing, you'll find a series of "Questions to Reflect Upon." Taking some time with these can assist you in drawing out and digesting what the writing means to you in this moment.

You'll also find a section called, "A Reminder to Myself" after each writing. This has been customized for each individual writing and will gently remind you of how far you've come in your journey and the progress you're continuing to make.

"A lot of people are crying out for help; they just don't know how to ask for it."

Gareth Michael

1

Moving from an Old Chapter to a New One

The idea of something coming to an end can bring up many emotions in you:

Fear ◦ Joy ◦ Happiness ◦ Anger ◦ Sadness ◦ Disgust Surprise ◦ Contempt ◦ Anticipation

Moving on from an old chapter to a new one can be one of the most exciting things you experience, yet it can also be one of the most daunting.

You can prepare for this change as much as you know how to; however, even when you've processed the idea of the change and the many different emotions that arise along with that, it never seems to be quite the same as going through the actual change itself.

Moving from one chapter to the next is one of the most natural parts of your journey and no different from each change that has happened before—you've grown from both the known and the unknown in your life.

It can be difficult to prepare for a change in your life because of the uncertainty about what's coming next. This uncertainty is what can make this process feel so hard.

This new chapter of your life will indeed contain many unknown factors, but it's important to remind yourself why you're making these changes to begin with.

It's easy for you to feel safe in the life you've spent so much time building in previous chapters, but, if you look back at your own life experiences, you'll see that whenever you've taken the first step into the unknown—even when it's been uncomfortable to do so—true growth always followed.

The reason this step can be so daunting is because only you can truly and deeply know the time you've spent creating this life for yourself, the challenges you've come through, and the internal strength that has come from this.

The changes that appear as your new chapter unfolds may also require that you deconstruct certain elements you've worked tirelessly to build or keep alive in the hope they'd last forever.

It's important to embrace the emotions that come along with change and to try your best not to judge or label them. Each experience is placed in front of you for a very special reason, even if this hasn't yet become fully apparent to you.

Everything you've been through has counted. It won't be forgotten, and it was never for nothing.

It can be hard to let go of the known and dive into the unknown, but this is the very nature of life.

What may help with this is acknowledging that the unknown aspects of life have allowed you to learn about the unknown parts of yourself, and this has allowed you to grow more than ever before.

Even though you've experienced many changes in your life, that doesn't mean any of these first steps into your next new beginning are any easier. Each new chapter pushes you to grow further, which is why they cannot be compared to each other. In simple terms, you've become a different person with each change.

When you finally feel ready to take the first step into your new chapter, the timing will be perfect for you.

Embrace each chapter, how much you've truly grown, the love you've been shown, and remember that each chapter has gifted you these experiences, which are uniquely your own.

Let's Take a Little Moment

Questions to Reflect Upon

1. What chapters in your life have you been happy or sad to say goodbye to?
2. What's the most recent chapter in your life you've had to move on from?
3. What are the different lessons each chapter has taught you?
4. What people have remained in your life throughout each of these chapters? What people are no longer part of your new chapter?
5. How have you changed as a person from one chapter to the next?
6. How do you feel about each of these changes?

A Reminder to Myself

♡ It's safe for me to keep on traveling down the path that feels right for me.

♡ I remain calm regardless of the situation, because I know in my heart it's happening for a reason—even when I find it difficult.

♡ It's safe for me to move on from my past and into the new chapter of my life.

♡ Whenever I step into the unknown, I know that, despite feeling uncomfortable, I'm truly growing.

♡ I'm learning to embrace all of my emotions without labeling or judging them.

♡ I know there's no chapter in my life that was ever without meaning or will ever be forgotten.

"Some of your biggest struggles
in life bring you toward your
biggest purpose in life."

Gareth Michael

2

Your Individual Path

Your individual path is an exquisitely beautiful and personal creation that's entirely unique to you. It can't be controlled, explained, copied, studied, or—often—even completely remembered.

Your journey is for you to live, to feel, to see, to explore, and, eventually, to leave.

Nobody truly knows what their path holds. Each individual begins their life by listening to how others live theirs, until eventually they start to see and feel how to live, guide, and shape their own.

It can be difficult or impossible to prepare for the routes presented to you, especially since it's guaranteed that nobody has ever walked in your footsteps before.

You meet many individuals who travel with you on your journey through life, just as you join others on theirs.

Some are with you from the beginning and stay with you until the end, some join you along the way for a period of time, and some decide to venture off in a different direction when they come to a crossroads.

You arrive at many crossroads throughout your life where you're faced with moments in which you need to make a decision. Some of these decisions are easy, some are challenging, some are big, and some are small, but all are part of your journey for a reason.

The one thing that's promised is there's no "wrong" path just as there's no way to define the "right" one.

Each path is filled with new experiences, new people, and new challenges that, at times, push you to your limits but also—and perhaps only after you've processed the sense of weakness you experienced—show you how strong you are.

There are other people in this world who go through similar experiences and patterns—people that you and many others are able to relate to.

This can be comforting and helpful in many ways, but the process of going through your own experiences is unique to you and holds lessons meant only for you.

Because your individual path is utterly your own and unlike any other, it can be difficult at times for people to understand some of the decisions you've made, even if you try to explain your perspective to them.

It's inevitable that others will compare your life to theirs and make assumptions about what you "should have done." This may feel frustrating, but understand that even if your journey includes certain experiences that have similarities to those of another, you're here to live your own life, not a version of anybody else's.

You can trust that any decision you've made was perfect for you, because it felt right at the time.

You're not here to explain yourself but simply to express yourself.

Trust your instincts, respect others' perspectives, and express yourself openly to loving people who are ready to listen.

Let's Take a Little Moment

Questions to Reflect Upon

1. Which person or people in your life had the biggest influence on you in shaping your own path in life?
2. Who do you know that's had experiences and patterns similar to yours?
3. Do you compare your life and path to others? If so, in what ways?
4. Can you think of a person or people whom you connected with in the "bad" times that made the "good" times even better?
5. Do you struggle to understand some of the decisions you've made?
6. What decisions have you made that you considered to be "wrong" or "right" for you? How do these decisions make you feel now?
7. Do you trust where your life is taking you?

A Reminder to Myself

♡ I have the ability to make changes in my life, as I always have options.

♡ Only I can feel my emotions. No one else can do it for me.

♡ Everything is working out for me now in ways that are perfect for me.

♡ I have the ability to learn about my mind and my emotions. I look forward to understanding myself, which will assist in understanding, connecting, and helping others.

♡ The only approval I'll ever need is my own.

"It's important that you listen to your own internal guidance about what feels right for you rather than just going with what you're told is right for you by any book, person, or theory."

Gareth Michael

3

Saying Goodbye

Saying goodbye to a loved one can be one of the most emotional experiences you'll ever go through. It can leave you feeling sadness, regret, shock, or, sometimes, even happiness or relief.

Whether the event was planned or not, nothing can prepare you for the emotions that will present themselves. You've never felt them before, and you hope never to feel them again.

Going from what was once such an exciting and apparently stable part of your life to saying goodbye—which always seemed so far away or which you believed you'd never have to say—can seem overwhelming.

As your body processes the shock, comfort and joy disappear, and it seems the color and light in the world have dimmed. Reality arrives, bringing with it difficult emotions.

Pain and sadness are all that remain, and you feel your heart will never be quite the same.

It can be hard to truly understand what a person means to you until you're forced to say goodbye.

Each person has a different relationship with, and reaction to, the emotions that arise when saying goodbye. Each person has their own way of processing, and sometimes that means not doing anything at all.

Just as there's no single body that's the same as another, there's no one emotion that will be felt in the exact same way by different people.

Each person needs a different amount of time to process a farewell. Many people may be willing to assist you, but nobody will be able to make these emotions disappear and, sometimes, talking about them can be too painful.

This can make it difficult to accept help from anyone, as you're not quite sure what part of you needs it—or even if you really want any help at all in this moment.

It takes time for the mind and body to emerge from shock, and this needs to happen before it's possible to process the emotions you're feeling.

This has never been an easy journey for any individual—as it requires exploring deep within yourself—and no one can do it for you. It's an unknown, arduous journey, and many aren't afforded the time to truly focus on it because they're hindered by their careers, responsibilities, family, friends, or even themselves.

Processing the experience of saying goodbye is often seen as necessary for only a specific period of time—when, in reality, it can have a lingering, ongoing effect on every area of your life.

Many are terrified of the thought of having to say goodbye to someone they love. Yet, when you're wrapped up in the process of saying goodbye, you may find you have just as strong a fear of coming fully out of that place and back into "normal life," where you'll have to begin interacting with the "real" world once again.

The realm of goodbye can become a safe space as much as it can be a painful one. At times, it's easier to stay with the pain, processing it only in small amounts, because it's a way of keeping that person in your life.

For many, the biggest fear is of accepting that your loved one is gone—of having to truly say goodbye.

It may seem that everything about your relationship with them could be forgotten, and the world could continue on as if they never existed even though they were such an important part of your life. How is that fair?

As painful as the emotion you're feeling truly is, it keeps them with you every single day.

However, if you're feeling this pain, the people around you are, too. This can create conflict, as those around you may want you to move on. They can never understand the depth of your emotion, and the fact that they're ready to move on can make you even less eager to do so. Only you truly know how important that relationship was. You don't want that flame to be extinguished.

You could find yourself in bittersweet limbo—you don't want to say goodbye, but you're not happy where you are.

When you say goodbye, everything within your life changes, because everything is affected by your relationship with the person and your relationship with yourself, your family, your friends, and your career.

You can't lie about what you're feeling, but everyone around you seems to be growing impatient that you let go and move on. It becomes easier to internalize or even suppress your feelings as a way to stop dealing with those emotions—to hide them and to hide from them.

But emotions that aren't acknowledged won't disappear. They'll ultimately force changes within you.

You may never have been advised or supported on how to fully process your emotions, but trust that it's entirely possible to do this—and doing so doesn't mean you'll ever forget your loved one.

Let's Take a Little Moment

Questions to Reflect Upon

1. Who comes to mind when you think of a time when you've had to say goodbye to someone? Picture that person in your mind.

2. Have you allowed your body the time it needed to process saying goodbye to this person?

3. Do you feel you've fully processed the emotions related to saying goodbye?

4. How long did it take for you to feel like yourself again, or have you ever?

5. Did you accept help during this difficult time, or did you do it on your own?

6. How has saying goodbye changed you as a person?

7. Do you wish things could have been different?

8. Do you have a fear of saying goodbye to others close to you in your life?

9. In what way did saying goodbye affect your other relationships and friendships?

10. Do you feel like you lost a part of yourself when you said goodbye?

A Reminder to Myself

♡ I'm constantly healing more than I thought and, for this, I'm grateful.

♡ I'm allowed to express pain. Just like everything else I feel, I'm feeling it for a reason.

♡ I believe in my ability to get through tough times. Whatever I manage to do today will be enough.

♡ I'm learning to spend time with my emotions, knowing they're going to help me with saying goodbye.

♡ At times, I may feel overwhelmed, but, deep down, I know I'm going to be okay.

♡ I'll allow my mind and my body the time they need to process all that's taking place.

♡ My heart may feel broken now but, over time, I know it will mend.

♡ I'll allow my healing process to continue for whatever amount of time is right for me.

"No one is able to feel the exact
emotions that you feel, even if they
say they feel them, too. Your emotions
are entirely unique to you."

Gareth Michael

4

Changing Life Patterns

How do you change something you've been
doing your entire life?

Can you accept that there are some areas of your life you may never be able to change? If not, what emotions well up in you as you consider this?

Not being in control of parts of your life can be a difficult concept to process, especially if you've spent years trying to change a pattern or an element of yourself but have seen little actual development. Or maybe you did see big progress at times, but, for some reason, at other times, those patterns came back.

If you can first come to a place where you can accept the patterns you've wanted to change for so long, that very acceptance can make a major difference in how you approach those patterns.

When a pattern—one that you've always disliked and wanted to change—becomes such an integral part of your life—something you're accustomed to living with day in and day out—a lot of emotion can become tangled up in it. In many situations, if that emotion itself is cleared, it can open the door for massive breakthroughs within you.

This may not always result in the outcome you expected, but it may result in something even better than what you once wished for.

Sometimes, not receiving what you wanted and, instead, having to go through an experience you didn't ask for can be a wonderful gift that blossoms from a pattern you weren't "allowed" to change for quite some time.

Many of the patterns you've been unable to change can force you to deal with emotions you didn't even know you had. They can also give you a different perspective on life and take the friendships and relationships around you into different territory, away from the places you once thought they were going.

Processing the emotions around these patterns can be hard, but it's never without purpose.

If you're looking to change life patterns that have become ingrained in you, it's inevitable that this change will shake up other areas of your life as well. Some changes may be easier than you thought they'd be, and some may be harder, but, as you work through them, you'll find you have all the support and strength you need within yourself.

Living with these types of patterns is a part of a normal life experience, and each person has their own view as to whether they're helpful or hurtful.

Though you may not have consciously chosen these patterns, and though you may not always have the ability to remove them, it's important to acknowledge that you do have the ability to view them for what they truly are. Ask yourself what they've taught you until now, what they're still teaching you in the present, and what they might be able to teach you in the future.

The one thing that tends to hold you back from trying to make changes is the emotion surrounding a particular pattern. Help yourself to clear the emotions clouding your life around this pattern. You can only receive this gift when you allow yourself to surrender—when you "give up" the fight against that emotion you were never able to control to begin with.

Accepting those emotions and dealing with them is no guarantee the pattern will change, but, once the emotion is cleared, your own perspective on the pattern will change. This is the greatest gift you can give yourself, and no one can force it on you.

Life can be full of mysteries. Some of your life's patterns will form a part of that mysterious and surprising journey. Some you'll be able to change, some you won't, some you'll see daily, and some you'll never see at all.

It's quite possible that what may need to change isn't the pattern itself but simply how you view it.

Let's Take a Little Moment

Questions to Reflect Upon

1. Can you accept that there are some areas of your life that you may not be able to change?

2. What do you feel holds you back from making a change?

3. Could a reluctance to feel your emotions be stopping you from making a positive change in your life?

4. What patterns within yourself have you not accepted? Why do you think you find it hard to accept them?

5. Are there others in your life stopping you from changing these patterns?

6. If you didn't have these patterns, how do you think your life would be different?

A Reminder to Myself

♡ I'm becoming a better version of myself with every passing day.

♡ I see my struggles as opportunities to learn and grow.

♡ Even if my patterns don't change, I know that how I view them definitely will.

♡ I accept that processing the emotions relating to my patterns can be hard at times, but it's not without purpose.

♡ I cherish the unique person that I am.

♡ I know all challenges are in my life to help me grow.

"Many would rather spend their time trying to change other peoples' patterns instead of spending time accepting and working on their own."

Gareth Michael

5

Aging

"Aging—the process of growing old."
- Oxford Dictionary

From your first breath, one simple process has been a constant part of your existence. Though you may be unaware of it for long periods of time, this process is always part of your journey, changing you as you go through each experience in life.

It's the one element that's always stable and guaranteed—the process of aging.

You've been aging from the very moment you were born. You may have viewed it positively, you may have viewed it negatively, or you may have been indifferent, but this process has continued with every heartbeat.

As every second passes, you naturally become a little older than you ever were before. This process has never been a secret, and it's something that happens before your very eyes.

If the process of aging is evident and inevitable, why do so many struggle with it?

What's your relationship with this word, this process?

Does it mean anything more to you now than it did a couple of seconds ago, a couple of months ago, a couple of years ago, or a couple of decades ago?

What's changed for you and within you during this time, and how do you think your relationship with this word will change for you as you continue to grow "older"—knowing there's nothing you can do to control this natural process other than to understand the way your mind perceives it?

As you were growing up, aging might have been described to you in many ways, and you were naturally surrounded by people from many age groups—from siblings to grandparents to aunts, uncles, and family friends.

Even so, you may not have considered the concept of aging at all until you had a direct experience that brought it to the front of your mind—maybe by witnessing the frailty of an older family member.

You may have been brought up in a family or a community where you were expected to accomplish key life goals by a certain age.

When you were younger, each of these key life stages might have seemed far away, and there seemed to be so much time before you had to act to make them a reality. But, in today's world, where your own voice and individuality are being taken into account more than ever, these expectations are no longer realistic.

This may become especially apparent at those times when you compare your life to those of older relatives or family friends when they were your age.

Your internal dialogue may begin:

- They were married by this age, but I'm not ready for that yet; I haven't found the one.
- They had a successful career at this age, and I'm still trying to figure out my path.
- They had a child, maybe more than one, by this age—how did they manage and balance it all?
- This was the age they became ill or started getting symptoms; I couldn't go through that kind of suffering now.
- This was the age they passed away; but they were so young, and they had so much more living to do.

Family and friends will often talk openly and willingly about the milestones they've achieved, but they may be less eager to discuss a topic like aging—which they could still be trying to come to terms with themselves.

How do you discuss something you can't control and that continues without your permission, triggering emotions that can be so difficult to understand? You spend your lifetime slowly becoming that older generation that once seemed so far away.

Despite how difficult it can sometimes be, communication is essential to understanding aging. If the conversation about aging is never opened, how will any generation going forward, including your own, ever truly be able to accept this process?

Whether you speak of it or not, aging is inevitable. But it's a process we can learn about and learn from by sharing with others, especially since aging means something unique and different to each individual.

Your own perspective may also change as each year passes and you notice changes in your appearance, your behaviors, and your body's capabilities. Letting others' perspectives inform you, and sharing with them in return, is a gift that can be passed on through the generations.

The natural process of aging occurs in every individual in every generation. Rather than pushing that idea away until you "have to deal with it," embrace the reality of aging and learn to understand it more deeply. Share with others this rich experience that all humans go through.

From the moment you started to read this writing to the moment you finished, you've aged. How does that make you feel?

Let's Take a Little Moment

Questions to Reflect Upon

1. What's your relationship with the process of aging?
2. Have you ever been surprised or even shocked by the aging process in yourself or another?
3. What part of aging concerns or scares you?
4. Is aging currently impacting your life? In what ways?
5. Have you found that your love for yourself has changed as you've aged? In what ways?
6. Do you think you have unrealistic expectations of what you should have achieved by your current age?
7. Do you find that you're putting more or less pressure on yourself as you get older?
8. How have your relationships changed as you've gotten older?
9. How has your relationship with your body changed as you've grown older?
10. As you've aged, what are the biggest things you've learned about yourself?

A Reminder to Myself

♡ I embrace the things I cannot change.

♡ I see changes as a welcome and normal part of my life.

♡ I understand that my mind, body, and emotions can give me everything I need for a happy life.

♡ I know that aging is inevitable, and I'm learning to accept it.

♡ I'm going through a natural part of what it means to be human.

♡ My self-worth isn't linked to my age.

♡ Aging has helped me learn a lot about myself.

"Whether it's intended or not, meeting your fears is often the quickest way to meet yourself."

Gareth Michael

6

Each Individual in Your Life Has Meaning

Throughout your life, from your very first breath, you've met many individuals—more than you'll ever be able to count or perfectly remember.

It can be challenging to truly understand the impact other individuals have had on you—and the impact you've had on them. Each interaction, each moment, and each person is a part of your journey, no matter what significance your mind finds in them at the time.

Whether you're aware of it or not, your mind registers every single interaction; therefore, each one has meaning. Just because you may not be able to identify that meaning doesn't mean it doesn't exist.

Think of all the individuals you know by name and see every day, every month, or every year, and then consider the many people you once knew who are no longer present in your life.

There are continuous interactions in your day-to-day life that you're unaware of—for example, the people you pass on the street as you do your errands or interact with only momentarily as you run from one responsibility to another.

Think of the many who come into your life each day—including those you haven't yet met who will play a part in your journey. Their role may be to redefine your present and give it new meaning, create joyful new memories, or even introduce new challenges.

The impact you have on another person, or their impact on you, occurs in the smallest and simplest of ways. Even those seemingly inconsequential, fleeting interactions—whether with people you know and trust or those you don't and may never get to know—can create a new memory or give you an unexpected perspective.

When has a new perspective, a wave of inspiration, or a deeply felt emotion ever been planned or expected? Whether these arise from your actions or from another's comment, behavior, or glance, this registers with you and has an impact.

Think of an individual in your life who's close to you, and review the life you've shared with them:

How they came into your life—where, when, and how you first met.

The ways in which they're still a part of your life—or, perhaps, why they're no longer a part of your life.

What they've taught you and what experiences with them you still feel grateful for or are working through.

How they changed you, how you've grown from knowing them, and how they might have grown from knowing you. There's a lot to think about. There's a lot of meaning.

Every individual is on their own unique journey. By simply being present, you can become a part of another's life path.

Some of the people who join you on your journey may teach you the biggest lessons of life, allowing you to feel emotions you didn't even know existed—both positive and negative. Others may bring up emotions in you that you may never feel again, and no label will be able to do justice to what you felt.

You'll never be able to control how people come into your life, but you can begin to understand that these encounters always have a purpose, because each person you meet in your life holds a lesson for you.

The gift is being able to look at the people who are part of your journey—the people in your past, the ones in your present, and the many you'll meet in the future—and appreciate how every one of those individuals contributes to shaping who you are.

In the same way, you bring meaning to each individual you meet—whether you try to or not—just by being yourself.

Let's Take a Little Moment

Questions to Reflect Upon

1. Which individuals do you feel have made the biggest impact on your life?
2. Can you think of individuals who continue to have an impact on your journey even though they're no longer with you?
3. What are the smallest interactions with others that have made the biggest impact on your life?
4. Do you think there's meaning behind every person who comes into your life?
5. Do you think you have the same level of impact on others as they have on you?

A Reminder to Myself

- ♡ I know I have the support of others.
- ♡ I freely give love to and accept love from those around me.
- ♡ I understand I'm on a journey with many others, and we all have things to teach each other.
- ♡ I accept and let go of those who've moved on from my life, and I'm grateful for their role in my journey.
- ♡ I accept that I have an impact on everyone I meet.
- ♡ I'm thankful to everyone I've met for helping to shape me as a person.

"You've never been able to control how individuals come in to your life, but you can begin to understand that this has never been without purpose."

Gareth Michael

7

Loving Yourself

Self-love is a journey, and it can take a lifetime to figure out what it truly means to you. There have likely been many times when you've been able to show yourself love in the moment, but there may have been just as many times when you've found it difficult to see your own worth and feel love for yourself.

You can spend hours, days, or years searching for a definition, a practice, a workshop, a book, a guru—anything that will enable you to love yourself continuously and freely as opposed to only in certain moments, and those often disappear as quickly as they arrived.

This search for self-love can be an emotional journey involving individuals who've been a consistent part of your life as well as those who've come and gone. On this journey, you may question what love truly means to you as you ponder the many ways in which you've felt love for another, from another, and for yourself.

Many people seek love from another person as validation that they're worthy of love and as a substitute for loving themselves. Although receiving love from another may be wonderful, it doesn't always lead to authentic self-love.

As you move along your path, you'll encounter individuals who see aspects of you that few—if any—others have seen. There are many reasons why you may feel able to open up and be yourself around certain individuals, though it may be hard to explain in words why this feels so natural.

This feeling—being yourself without having to try, allowing those people to see you for who you truly are—can be a place where you're comfortable enough to be both vulnerable and happy at the same time. It's in this space that those people can also easily accept those qualities within you that you might have spent years battling to accept in yourself.

What you're feeling in this situation with another is an unparalleled sense of acceptance. However, a part of your journey may also involve seeing those people leave—taking with them your sense of security about the love they held for you and your qualities.

This can be difficult, but, by going through this separation, you can truly let go of the crutch of another person's perspective and begin your own self-created experience of valuing these aspects of who you are.

An important part of why those individuals were in your life was to show you that they were able to love these qualities and, therefore, so can you.

Self-love is something you can learn to understand on a logical level, but nobody can teach you to feel it internally. Only your own personal journey can show you this, as each person's journey towards self-love is unique to them.

Love can be one of the hardest things to show yourself. Some try in vain to find a way to love themselves by experiencing it through another; but only through holding that love for yourself can it become a steady and consistent part of your life.

Self-love is being patient with yourself on the days you're feeling short-tempered.

Self-love is expressing your emotions even when they're hard to put into words.

Self-love is loving the body you're in while accepting you may not always find it easy to look at.

Self-love is being your authentic self—being true to who are and how you feel.

Love truly flourishes when you're able to love your own qualities and appreciate the opportunity of sharing this love with another.

Let's Take a Little Moment

Questions to Reflect Upon

1. What does self-love mean to you?
2. How has your relationship with self-love changed over the years?
3. Do you think your sense of self-love is ever conditional upon other people's views or opinions? In what ways?
4. What are the parts of you that you love the most?
5. What are the parts of you that you feel you're still working on?
6. How do you think your life would be different if you could love every part of you?
7. Have you ever relied on another to experience self-love?

A Reminder to Myself

♡ I deserve to forgive, to be forgiven, to be heard, and to be understood.

♡ I love myself, and I know that I deserve to be happy.

♡ It's okay to feel all of my emotions—the "good" and the "bad"—knowing that I'm always full of love.

♡ The only approval I'll ever need is my own.

♡ I love my body, mind, and emotions, and all they do for me.

♡ The more I love myself, the more I can share this love with another.

♡ I'm on a journey of self-love that changes day by day.

"The process of learning to love yourself deeply includes facing any thoughts about why you feel you shouldn't be loved."

Gareth Michael

8

Nature

"Nature—the phenomena of the physical world collectively, including plants, animals, the landscape, and other features and products of the earth, as opposed to humans or human creations."
- Oxford Dictionary

Nature impacts you as an individual more than you'll ever know.

It's not just something you see when you're outside—
It's a part of each breath you take,
each blink of your eyes,
each tear that forms, and
each hair that grows.

In the past—and, at times, even now in the present—you may have told yourself that you'd like to spend more time reconnecting with Nature and with yourself. That can mean something different for each individual, but it usually means taking time out of your busy, day-to-day schedule and spending time with Nature itself.

Or you may be spending time in Nature already without fully comprehending the magnificence of a small part of what Nature has already created—you!

It's understandable why the world views humans and Nature as different and separate.

But that makes it easy to forget that each individual is still one of the many creations of the Earth, all of which contribute to the mysterious and encompassing phenomenon that is Nature.

When you allow yourself the time to look at how you view Nature, you naturally become aware of any separation that you yourself have felt from it.

By embracing this inquiry, you may once again begin to perceive humanity—which includes you—and Nature as one, as has always been the case.

You may have sensed this divide between humanity and Nature for any number of reasons—reasons that, at times, have been outside of your control, whether they be personal pressures, work stresses, or simply due to a perspective you may never have had before.

Even with your busy schedule, you have within you the ability to effortlessly feel a connection to something you're already very much enmeshed in.

You can do this without having to "disconnect" from your everyday world in order to "reconnect" with Nature—because you're a part of Nature, and Nature is a part of you.

Stemming from this simple understanding, you may be able to contemplate—

A simple plant in your office,
the garden at your home,
a forest you drive through,
the mountains or the sea on television,
the animals present in your life,
or even an individual you meet,

and be able to feel a deeper connection, a love for what Nature truly represents—a greater, grander existence that you, everyone around you, and everything you see are equally a part of.

All are living a life as vivid and complex as your own. This can be deeply comforting in a world—and sometimes within your own mind—that's filled with chaos. It yields the realization that you're not on your own.

Let's Take a Little Moment

Questions to Reflect Upon

1. What does the word "Nature" mean to you?
2. At what times and in what ways do you feel connected with Nature?
3. What memories do you have of spending time in Nature?
4. What elements of Nature do you most value?
5. Do you think that your life or your actions impact Nature? In what ways?
6. How can you find more time to spend in Nature? Do you feel like you want to?

A Reminder to Myself

♡ I now feel I'm connected to Nature more than I ever thought or knew.

♡ I'll find a way to spend more time in Nature.

♡ I'm one with Nature. Nature is around me everywhere I go.

♡ Nature gives me many things in my life, so I'll make the time to give back to it.

♡ I appreciate all the natural beauty in my life.

"Nature is something that impacts
you more than you'll ever know."

Gareth–Michael

9

Confidence

*"Confidence—a feeling of self-assurance arising from
an appreciation of one's own abilities or qualities."*
– Oxford Dictionary

You may have noticed there are some areas of your life in which you feel confident and other areas in which you don't.

When you're lacking confidence, what are the emotions you experience?

Perhaps you have feelings of sadness, self-pity, uselessness, unworthiness, failure.

Maybe you compare yourself to another, looking at their life and seeing them succeed effortlessly in a certain area. Yet, for some reason, no matter how much effort you put into it, you haven't been able to develop that same skill in the way you'd like or been able to incorporate what you've been taught.

When you're feeling a lack of confidence about something, it can weigh heavily on you. Much of the time, the feeling of lacking in a particular area may affect you more than your lack of skill in the activity itself.

That feeling is often linked to a part of you that wants to prove something to yourself or to others.

It also stops you from actually seeing the growth within yourself, because you may be constantly comparing yourself to others, and that can blind you from seeing how far you've genuinely come.

Maybe you only feel the confidence you desire when you receive recognition from another—when you hear they were "impressed" by or "proud" of you for what you've accomplished. Or you may only feel confident when your achievements are equal to or even "better" than what the person you've been comparing yourself to has achieved.

But how and when does this pattern of comparing yourself to others stop, and how does confidence more naturally increase instead of you having to work hard to try to create it and maintain it?

First, it's necessary to understand that confidence always starts with you. It isn't established as the result of another's opinion about you, even though praise always feels good.

Confidence stems from the process of looking directly at each of the areas of your life that you deem as strengths and weaknesses and then sitting with the feelings they present to you.

Sitting with these emotions, even the negative ones, doesn't prolong or enhance them; instead, this process allows you to address the feelings for what they are.

Whereas, in the past, it may have taken a long period of time to work through one of these emotions—or you may have even tried to suppress it—now you can feel it fully, understanding it for what it actually is and not what you may have built it up to be.

In some areas in which you're lacking confidence, you may have memories of a situation or circumstance where that confidence was knocked down. You may not be able to change the past, but you can sit with the feelings in the present and express them freely in your own safe environment.

This is the first step in the process—identifying and owning memories and emotions you may have previously only chosen to look at when you were forced to or triggered.

When you make the commitment to yourself to begin looking at these feelings, spend time with them, and engage the memories you feel are affecting your confidence, you won't experience the feelings in the same way as before, because you're giving yourself space to look at them for what they are.

You can truly know these experiences no longer define you but have existed within you for a reason.

They're a part of your experience, and you'll grow from them, just as you have from every other challenge that's come before.

Let's Take a Little Moment

Questions to Reflect Upon

1. What's your relationship with confidence?
2. What's your first memory of having your confidence shaken?
3. Do you think your life would be different if you had more confidence? In what ways?
4. How do you feel in those times when you struggle with confidence?
5. Which individuals in your life tend to shake your confidence? And who helps to grow your confidence?

A Reminder to Myself

♡ I've come so far and been through so much, and, because of this, I believe in myself more than ever before.

♡ I've made it through difficult times, therefore I know I'm going to make it through this.

♡ As I continue to grow as a person, my confidence will continue to grow, too.

♡ The tough times I'm experiencing will be behind me one day, and they'll have played a vital role in the person I'll become. For that, I'm grateful.

♡ In any moment when I lack in confidence, I know it won't last forever.

♡ I know that taking the time to understand why I lack confidence will help me to discover the inner confidence I always knew I had.

"Many spend their lifetime feeling their voice isn't being heard. It's important to start listening to your own voice first—to love it, understand it, cherish it. Only then will the world be truly ready to listen."

Gareth Michael

10

One Step at a Time

All you can ever do is take the first step.

Any step forward is new and unknown, and any first step can feel daunting. At times, such a step may introduce new emotions you've never felt before. At other times, it may bring new meaning and definition to emotions you've known your entire life—emotions you enjoy and would usually want to feel but that could, in this instance, seem overwhelming.

Or it could bring up issues or emotions you've been taught your entire life to push away—to the point that the effort brings you to tears.

Every step you take signifies growth, though at times it may be hard to see that clearly, especially when so many different emotions arise.

Emotions can be more present during these times of moving forward and experiencing change, but this is the natural way in which you continue to develop trust within yourself. Developing trust and understanding that emotions will be with you each step of the way—as your own personal guides—is part of this growth.

Listening to your emotions, no matter what they are, can be just as important as taking the step itself.

There may be a part of you that feels fully ready for this first step, but there may also be a part of you that feels scared. These feelings exist to challenge you, because only you will know, within your heart, when the urge to take the step becomes stronger than your fear of the emotions that may come when you finally do so.

There's no right or wrong answer, no perfect advice that will allow you to take that first step. It has to feel right from within yourself.

When that right time comes, it's important to communicate with yourself and address everything you're truly feeling as well as to communicate with others whom you love and trust.

Sometimes, before or after you take a first step, you may feel you're standing still and have no direction. This is a necessary phase in the process in which you're keeping your two feet on the ground and finding your balance, however long that may take.

This pause between steps may occur many times throughout your life. It allows you to find your true self instead of feeling like you're living a version of yourself.

There's no way to accurately predict when you'll be able to lift your foot off the ground and step forward into the life you're now ready for. Yet, this first step is always perfectly timed. Even as you start your new chapter, you may need a period of time to understand the changes that are taking place and how they'll affect the life you've known for so long.

Many people beat themselves up about not taking the next step when, in reality, it isn't the right time for them yet. The only way to take the step is to listen to yourself.

While "taking action" is often viewed as an indication of strength, there's an equal amount of strength in simply listening to yourself and understanding when it's not the time to take action. What works for you may not be what works for someone else.

Understand that it's the ability to listen to yourself that takes true strength, whether you end up taking a step or not.

Let's Take a Little Moment

Questions to Reflect Upon

1. What's the biggest step you feel you've taken in your life to date?

2. What's the next step that you're considering taking? Is there anything stopping you from taking this step?

3. What emotions do you feel when you consider taking this step?

4. How have you changed or grown as a person since you last took a step forward?

5. What do you feel you could gain by taking this step? What do you feel you could potentially lose?

6. What does this next step mean to you?

7. Do you feel you have the support you need to take this step?

A Reminder to Myself

♡ I know in my heart that each step in my life is happening for a reason—even when I find it difficult.

♡ Each step is helping me to understand, and build a relationship with, my emotions.

♡ I can let go of people who no longer have my best interests at heart.

♡ I trust each step I take and know that the timing is always right for me.

♡ Every step I take is different from the last, because I'm constantly changing and evolving.

♡ Each step I take gives me strength and understanding and, for this, I'm grateful.

"It's easier to understand what you're
going through in the present when
you take the time to understand
what you went through in the past
and why you went through it."

Gareth Michael

11

The "Perfect" Relationship

Every person dreams of the "perfect" relationship. You may desire it in many areas of your life—the love and support of a partner; open communication with and unconditional love from your children, your parents, your siblings, and your friends; or even a balanced relationship between your career and your personal life.

"Perfect," for many people, is defined as having all the desirable elements, qualities, or characteristics conveyed through television or social media, encouraged by the pressures of society, or drawn from experiences and memories you've defined as perfect throughout your own life.

Past experiences, in particular, may have a significant impact on what you define as perfect in each of the relationships mentioned above.

You may have fond memories of certain elements of your life, memories that make you seek to recreate new variations of these experiences, again and again, to share with others and to enjoy yourself.

You may also have had experiences in your life that were far from enjoyable and that motivated you to do the opposite of what you were shown then in an effort to ensure those experiences wouldn't be repeated.

Or you may find yourself in the same unwanted position again and again simply because it's all you've ever known.

Those who continuously strive for perfection tend to suppress their emotions, pushing them aside in the pursuit of a better life—one they may never have had.

In some cases, they briefly experienced this "ideal life" at one point in the past, and now they have an internalized expectation that they'll be able to deliver that same ideal life to others—whether to their children, their family, or other people whom they care for.

They may pressure themselves to provide this life to their loved ones and try to do so by recreating those rose-tinted memories—even if their loved ones aren't interested in their vision of perfection or find it confusing or restricting.

In search of relationship perfection, many people spend time trying to change the behavior of those around them. This is inevitably an almost impossible task, especially if the individuals being focused upon have no intention of changing or simply aren't capable of change.

The perfect relationship, in any area of your life, can only truly begin when you're able to recognize it doesn't exist—that the concept of perfection is completely subjective, unique to each person, and changes over time.

Most importantly, it has to start with developing your own concept of what the perfect relationship with yourself looks like.

This is where you can shine a light on old mindsets—personal images influenced by television, social media, the pressures of society, or the memories you've defined as perfect from your own life—and allow them to dissolve or evolve, one step at a time.

This isn't something that can be achieved solely by yourself, because you only have access to one perspective—your own. Accepting the limitations of this perspective can help you to build a healthier relationship with yourself.

The perfect relationship doesn't mean being able to completely rely on yourself or to completely rely on another. It means being open and vulnerable, and trusting that throughout your life, you'll do both.

When you look at the efforts you've made to create perfect relationships in the different areas of your life, do you feel you've been putting the same amount of time and dedication into your relationship with yourself?

Perhaps you've given up on this, believing it could never be perfect, no matter how hard you try.

There's no such thing as perfect, there's only authentic. Once you have an open and honest relationship with yourself and others, you'll stop trying to achieve perfection and enjoy the richness of being your authentic self.

Let's Take a Little Moment

Questions to Reflect Upon

1. What are your expectations of what a perfect relationship looks like for you?
2. Do you feel you have the perfect relationship with yourself?
3. Who do you want a perfect relationship with?
4. Do you feel there's anything holding you back from having open and honest relationships?
5. Have you ever come close to having the perfect relationship with yourself or with others?
6. Have you ever sacrificed parts of yourself in searching for the perfect relationship?

A Reminder to Myself

♡ I know I have the strength to walk away when a person or a situation isn't healthy for me.

♡ Nothing stands in the way of me loving myself.

♡ My emotions allow me to learn more about myself. I know it's okay to express all of my emotions—even the ones I've been taught not to.

♡ I'll develop an authentic relationship with myself before developing them with others.

♡ I understand that my relationships are forever changing and evolving.

"When communication breaks down
in a relationship, you're no longer
growing together. You've started
the process of growing apart."

Gareth Michael

12

A Single Moment

Have you ever considered how
important a moment can be?

I n a single moment, everything can change.

There are moments in life you wish to remember forever, there are moments in life you wish to forget, there are moments in life you look forward to, there are moments in life you spend looking into the past, and there are moments when you simply find yourself in the present.

Why do some moments stand out so much more vividly than others?

A moment is defined as a very brief period of time, yet some moments connect you to a part of yourself where words cease to exist.

Within those moments, you experience deep emotions or, sometimes, a space where no emotions are present at all—simply the still feeling of serenity.

In these moments, something registers within you that stands out from the other 86,399 seconds of the day and the endless thoughts that don't resonate as powerfully.

There's a beautiful feeling to those moments when you're simply present, being yourself without trying, and you realize you understand something differently.

You've gained a new perspective.

It can happen anytime or anywhere: You could be deep in thought, alone in Nature, or in communication with another.

These particular moments cannot be forced nor do they always need to be studied, but they're worthy of acknowledgment for the impact they have.

In one moment, you have all the money you need and, in the next moment, it's gone.

In one moment, you have perfect health and, in the next moment, it changes in a way you couldn't have been prepared for.

In one moment, you have the loving relationship you've always dreamed of with another and, in the next moment, you're on your own, coming to terms with being in a relationship with only yourself.

In one moment, you open your eyes for the first time and, in another moment, you finally close them for good.

A moment may have a strict definition, but what does it mean to you? Each one contains emotions, thoughts, memories, and more.

Trust that whatever that moment represents for you today is exactly what it's supposed to represent.

Your understanding of any moment will inevitably change and evolve over time, yielding new understanding and insights, and each of those meanings is perfect.

Each experience you've lived through, each person you've met, and the times you've spent with yourself, listened to yourself, and loved yourself have molded you into the person you are in this moment.

As you now sit and read these words, the world continues to flow and move around you as it always has and always will.

Yet, by taking the time to read this writing, you could be creating a memorable moment for yourself that will influence all the moments to come.

Let's Take a Little Moment

Questions to Reflect Upon

1. What moments have had the biggest impacts in defining your life?

2. What emotions did you feel within these moments that made them stand out?

3. Who's been most present with you in these moments throughout your life?

4. Do you remember these moments as mostly positive or negative?

5. What can you learn from previous moments to help you with the future ones?

6. How do you feel about the moments yet to come that will impact your life?

A Reminder to Myself

♡ I'm on a journey to understand my feelings and emotions. It can be a rollercoaster, but I know it's worth it.

♡ Everything is working out for me now in ways that are perfect for me, even if I don't always see it clearly.

♡ I have the ability to make changes—I know I have more options than are apparent in this moment.

♡ I understand and accept that everything can change within a moment.

♡ I know that, even when I'm feeling down, it won't last forever.

"Finding love for who you were in
the past is key to understanding how
to love yourself in the present."

Gareth Michael

13

What's Your Reality?

"Reality—the state of things as they actually exist, as opposed to an idealistic or notional idea of them."
- Oxford Dictionary

As an individual, you have your own definition of what reality is, and this interpretation impacts each decision you make in life, each mindset you have, and even determines who you choose to surround yourself with in your day-to-day life.

Your definition of reality and your view of the world have changed drastically since you were a child, and each change has had a major impact on you. The impact may not always have been visibly noticed or deeply analyzed, but each shift has truly changed how you live your life.

While you were developing as a child and throughout your teenage years, you may have been shown practical examples and taught what was considered "right," what was considered "wrong," what was "real," and what was "fake."

As you grew from a teenager into a young adult, life often presented you with experiences that were unexpected, and each one challenged your sense of reality relative to what you'd been taught.

As you began to live your own life and accumulated your own experiences, your version of reality changed deeply from how you perceived it as a child, and this reality may have been very different from what the people around you said it was.

This evolution in your perspective can lead to a place where you feel free from the reality you were taught and shown previously. Or, it can bring you to a place of confusion, because this place is different from everything you knew before—it's a completely new reality for you.

When there are even slight changes within what you consider your reality, it forces you to ask the question: "If my reality changed once, will it change again?"

No version of reality is right or wrong, and it's important to understand, though you may not realize it, that you have many definitions and versions of your own reality.

It's vital to explore your own current version of reality before you begin to explore or provide perspectives on anyone else's. If you feel unable to explain or understand your own reality, it might be difficult to offer guidance on another's.

Bear in mind that the reality of what you believe about an individual and the reality they believe to be true—which they probably don't show you—might be very different. Yet, each of these realities is true for each of you. Neither is right or wrong; they're simply the perspective that each person has.

Just as others' realities are different than yours, you might investigate your own reality to better understand how it's evolved over the course of your lifetime.

Ask yourself how the various influences, lessons, and perspectives that have come to you over the course of your life helped shape your reality into what you know it to be today.

Can you look back, without judgment, at a time in your life and honestly say your reality wasn't different then, even in small ways?

With the benefit of perspective, you can acknowledge that previous reality was who you were in that part of your life; it was your reality at the time, because it felt right and was true for you. It may not be your reality anymore.

For many individuals, there are primarily two types of reality: There's the reality you see yourself living each day—one that likely hasn't changed for an extended period of your life.

And then there's the other reality—the part of yourself you may not be willing or able to look at too closely, because accepting it may involve making changes you've been too fearful to even consider.

When your mind can't predict the outcome in your life of that shift in perspective, it may feel safer and easier to remain where you are, even though you know, deep inside, it's not the place where you'll be able to grow, flourish, and be happy.

Your reality is based upon the things you see, hear, and believe. Interestingly, it's also made up of the many things you don't want to see or believe, the voices you don't wish to hear, or the numerous other things you can't even dare to think about. All of these come together to create your own personal reality of where you are in your life at this moment.

Many people live the life that was planned out for them, even though they know this life doesn't accurately reflect who they truly are or what they need in this moment.

Still, they try to make it work, because it's the only reality they know—the one they're comfortable with. Any change in what you've known for a large portion of your life can bring up intimidating emotions, and these can make it difficult to challenge your own version of reality—even if somewhere inside you know it has to change.

Is your reality the version of yourself that knows changes need to be made, or is your reality the version of yourself that functions without question each day? Or are these both part of the same thread?

There may be a step forward that you know is right for you, because you can no longer live the way you have been. But the reality of making the change and taking the step itself—as well as dealing with all the emotions that come along with that—may seem too difficult to handle.

It can be hard to challenge something that's been real for you for so long, but the fact that you now feel a need to do so—when, for a long period of your life, you didn't—means you genuinely know it's time to take this step.

Let's Take a Little Moment

Questions to Reflect Upon

1. Which people in your life have helped to form your reality?
2. Who primarily taught you your sense of right and wrong?
3. What are the experiences in your life that have had the biggest impact in defining you and your reality?
4. How has your reality changed in the last 10 years, if at all?
5. How different is your reality from that of others in your family? Can you understand the origins of their reality?

A Reminder to Myself

- ♡ As I grow and change, so too does my sense of reality.
- ♡ I've let go of needing to do things a certain way. I'm learning that life is forever evolving, and I'm always learning and growing with it.
- ♡ I allow others the freedom to live their lives as they see fit.
- ♡ It's okay if people don't understand my reality—what's important is that I'm comfortable with it.
- ♡ Change helps me to realize my potential. It allows me to see the person I was in the past, to accept the person I am now, and to embrace the person I'm becoming.

"How you deal with any challenges that are yet to come will be based entirely upon the many things you've learned, or not learned, from your past."

Gareth Michael

14

A Difficult Life

There are few individuals who view the entirety of their lives as having been easy. Each person has a different background, a different path, a different way of communicating, and different ways they experience and express emotions.

You're unique beyond what the mind can begin to comprehend, and you have your own particular conception of what you find easy and what you consider difficult.

Throughout your life, you've undoubtedly experienced many challenges. Some of these have challenged you mentally, and some have challenged you physically or emotionally, too. What you may struggle to truly see is the strength that's developed within you as a result of those difficult experiences.

Something you may have difficulty with at one point in your life may no longer feel difficult later on due to the experience you gained the first time.

On the other hand, if you still haven't fully dealt with the emotions that arose during the first experience, that can make it even more difficult the second time. This is because you're not only still trying to process those previous emotions, but you're now also experiencing new versions of them.

Your emotional responses change and develop as you grow and experience new things throughout life. This is why no emotion can be explained in just one or two words. They, and your responses to them, evolve as you continue to go through good and bad experiences.

Why does it seem we spend more time discussing the difficult periods as opposed to the fun and enjoyable times?

The difficulties of life seem to be an area in which people feel they can most easily relate to one another. Almost everyone has experienced the loss of a loved one, illness, heartache, or money issues.

Sharing those experiences can provide a sense of unity, love, and support, whereas people can't always relate to the successes that others have in life, or they may even feel envy or resentment toward those who seem more fortunate.

At times, the sharing of a positive experience can actually create separation, jealousy, and discontent.

Another reason people may want to discuss the more difficult times is because they've learned more from these experiences than from the "successful" moments in life.

After each difficult episode you go through, why does it often seem there's another one right around the corner?

Picture your life as if you'd lived it without any difficulty—from the moment you were born until you grew into the person reading these words right now.

Ask yourself these questions: "How different would my life be without any of those challenges? How different would my relationship be with myself, with my partner, my best friend, my family, my career?"

Even though most people may wish for change in many areas of their lives, they may never take the time to understand how these changes would actually impact so many other aspects of their lives in addition to the specific element they're finding difficult in the moment.

Neither extreme of experience—constant ease nor endless struggle—is beneficial all the time, which is why, throughout your life, you experience elements of both in varying degrees.

Everyone learns from both the challenging and the enjoyable moments in their life; it's by living through both that the entire range of emotions is experienced.

Life continuously presents new challenges of all different kinds and from many different angles, and this can cause the mind to panic at times.

This feeling of panic is urging you to address the fear that's been brought up in you. It's important to be open to addressing your fear and looking at it directly, whatever it may be.

When you're strong enough to do this, the solution to—and the meaning of—the experience will present itself.

With each challenge you face, you're given the opportunity to truly grow. This is especially true when you don't feel you have the strength for this or when it feels like another challenge is the last thing you need.

Remember that your path is perfect for what you're here to experience and to show you how strong you truly are. Through these challenges, everyone naturally adapts and evolves.

You're not the same person you were a year ago or a day ago; you're the person you're meant to be right now, with more strength and love than ever before.

Let's Take a Little Moment

Questions to Reflect Upon

1. What would you define as the most difficult parts of your life?

2. Do you view other people's lives as being less or more difficult than your own? If so, in what ways?

3. Which difficult elements of your life do you feel you're still processing?

4. What emotions are brought up when you encounter something difficult?

5. Do you share and express your difficult times with others?

6. How have you made it through difficult times in the past?

7. Do you feel supported through difficult times?

8. Are you kind to yourself or hard on yourself during these times?

9. How have difficult times shaped and changed you as a person?

A Reminder to Myself

♡ I forgive myself for the times I've thought I wasn't good enough.

♡ In difficult times, I'm willing to feel challenging emotions, understand them, grow from them, and let them go.

♡ I accept myself during those times when I feel overwhelmed and frustrated.

♡ I continue to process and let go of any resistance I have to asking others for help.

♡ I understand everyone faces challenging times and that it's important to give support to others and also to accept support myself.

"Every challenge helps develop your understanding of your own life—and the unique lessons it holds only for you."

Gareth Michael

15

Change Is Inevitable

Change may be experienced at any time in many different areas of your life. Change can be difficult, because it may feel like you're losing control of something you've spent a long time getting comfortable with.

Each change naturally brings with it an uncertainty about what's to come and, even if you know the change is necessary, it doesn't always make the process any easier or make you feel more secure about it.

Change can mean many things, and people have mixed emotions about change.

In every year of your life so far, there have been so many memories associated with change that it's difficult to even work out how you felt about them. Each change you've experienced may elicit a combination of positive and negative feelings.

However, as you look at your own life, you'll see that change has always naturally taken place—whether you initiated it or not—and you've learned something new each time.

At times, it may seem easier to say no to certain changes, because they can force you out of your comfort zone.

It's easier and more comfortable to look into the past and remember changes that have already happened, because you're viewing them from a secure place where you can clearly see the positive results those challenges brought with them.

By contrast, new change brings new challenges. When facing potential changes, whether today or in the near future, it's much more difficult to see the possible benefits that could result from embracing them.

That's why change can be so intimidating; saying no to change often stems from wanting to stay in a safe place.

Sometimes, saying no to change may inadvertently put you into a "limbo" space where you feel unhappy with your current situation, but you may believe that making even the smallest change may impact areas of your life that you want to stay as they are. Therefore, it feels easier and safer not to make any change at all.

Or you may feel you have enough going on in your life without creating more work and stress for yourself.

Even if a change was guaranteed to bring a positive outcome, you might still ask yourself if it was worth the effort due to the amount of time you'd need to spend developing it and making it happen.

Change can also force you to consider areas of your life that you'd been waiting for the "right time" to address.

It can cause elements you'd been neglecting to get pushed to the forefront, whether you like it or not.

Nobody likes being forced into a position they didn't choose, even if it's life putting you in this position rather than any one particular individual.

Each person likes to think they're in control and will make changes when they decide to.

Changes come about in a number of ways, including:

- a change you want to make;
- a change made by another that results in a change for you, too; and
- a change you feel is forced upon you or a situation that can no longer go unaddressed.

No matter how change enters your life, and no matter what it might mean to you, it will present challenges. But what's guaranteed is that change only comes into your life when you're strong enough to deal with it.

Most of the time, you won't feel that way when it's happening, because the change itself shows you an inner strength you didn't know you had. Or it may be displaying your inner strength to another who needed to see it.

There may be many areas of your life you feel grateful for, but there also may be areas you want to change.

As you address the challenges that inevitably come with change, you grow in ways you may not have felt prepared for.

That's what makes the experience difficult—but it's also what makes it so worthwhile.

As you process the emotions that naturally arise with change, what may at first seem a negative experience will, over time, turn into a positive one.

Let's Take a Little Moment

Questions to Reflect Upon

1. When you think of unexpected changes that have happened in your life, do you think of them positively or negatively?
2. How do you feel when change occurs in your life?
3. What are the events in your life that have changed you most as a person?
4. Have you ever tried to stop changes from happening?
5. When was the last time a major change occurred in your life?
6. What part of you looks forward to change, and what part fears it?
7. How has change benefited you in the past?
8. Do you feel you were ever forced to change? How did that impact you emotionally?

A Reminder to Myself

♡ I value change for helping me realize my vast potential.

♡ I'm open to change, and I welcome it into my life.

♡ I appreciate that the small "setbacks" change often presents help me to grow in ways I couldn't have imagined.

♡ Change is always occurring, even when I'm unaware of it.

♡ I cannot control everything. Honestly, how much control have I ever really had?

"There are many things in life you can try to run away from, but one thing you can never run away from is yourself."

Gareth Michael

16

What Does Family Mean to You?

"Family—a group consisting of two parents and
their children living together as a unit."
- Oxford Dictionary

Over the years, the meaning of family has changed and been challenged by many people around the world. If you've seen your own family change over the years, that may mean your definition of family has also changed.

The word "family" is often strongly linked to the word "home," the place where so many memories of your childhood were formed.

Maybe, even to this day, the thought of home can make you laugh or bring you to tears.

It can summon thoughts of people that made you feel a world of emotions, both happy and painful.

There are countless families around the world, and each one is unique. There might be similarities between how you and others define family, but the impact of your family on you—in the past, the present, and the future—isn't the same as the impact the families of others have on them.

For many, family is represented by the way certain individuals make them feel—including the support and unconditional love given by parents, siblings, uncles, aunts, cousins, and friends.

But for others, the thought of family triggers memories that justify why they left home to begin with.

Many think of family members as being committed to supporting each other through the positive and negative times, both as individuals and together as a unit.

Others find it an ongoing battle to try to understand and love the people in their families and, often, they're not completely sure why family members made certain decisions.

If an individual has been forced into this place throughout their life due to their role within the family, it's understandable why the idea of family may cause them to feel conflicting or even hostile emotions.

In addition to your biological family—and often because of positive and negative experiences with biological family members—you may regard certain friends or anyone you feel a close connection to as family. This can provide a broader view of how many family members you truly have and can also bring more family into your life than you thought possible.

Each family you're a part of is important and special in its own way. With or without biological ties, family represents a group of people who stand with each other during the best of times and also during the toughest of times because of the connection and love they feel for one another.

This doesn't mean there aren't sometimes disagreements or decisions made that hurt members of any kind of family. However, with communication among parties who disagree and mutual respect for the love they have for one another, solutions will present themselves.

It's important that each individual be honest about how they're feeling and understand that each person is capable of creating the same situations or "mistakes" as another.

This doesn't mean you forget the issue; it simply allows you to release the emotion of what you're feeling and learn from the experience itself.

Being able to forgive a family member for an action that hurts you—or one that may have hurt you in the past—can be difficult. However, forgiving someone opens you to an understanding of why they took that action, allows the family to learn from this experience, and creates a stronger bond with everyone involved.

When you act using communication and understanding, a negative experience can turn into a positive one that strengthens the bond of love that holds the family together.

Let's Take a Little Moment

Questions to Reflect Upon

1. What does family mean to you?
2. What memories or places come to mind when you hear the word "home?" How do these make you feel?
3. Do you wish you could spend more time with your family? Which family member do you have the closest bond with?
4. Are you at ease when you spend time with your family? In what ways do you feel supported by them?
5. When has your family challenged you the most?
6. Do you think of family as including those outside of your biological family?
7. Do you have good communication with your family?

A Reminder to Myself

♡ My family is always assisting me with my growth, even when I find it challenging.

♡ I'm learning to express things firstly to myself. I know that expressing to the people I love will follow when the time is right for me.

♡ I appreciate and support those closest to me for who they are.

♡ I accept that many situations are out of my control. These often present an opportunity to learn more about myself, my emotions, and my reactions.

♡ The relationships within my family will continue to evolve and change—as will I.

"When you become the love of your own life, your happiness is no longer reliant on others."

Gareth Michael

17

Trust

"Trust—the firm belief in the reliability, truth,
or ability of someone or something."
- Oxford Dictionary

Trust isn't a concept that's easily defined, as it means something different to each person. You probably have people in your life you know you can trust because they've been with you as long as you can remember, or you've come through many challenges together.

In the same way that you can't truly be taught to love someone, you also can't be convinced by another person that someone is trustworthy.

Trust is something that's established over a period of time; it can't be forced.

When you were developing from a child into a young adult, many of the definitions and principles you'd previously absorbed might have begun to change.

As you continue to go through life, you may question the journey itself and what it means to you. This may bring up issues that cause you to question yourself or another. The foundations that once seemed so secure may begin to crack, and your previous understanding of trust may no longer be valid for what you're here to experience.

Your ability to trust others is a fundamental part of who you are in this moment and of the person you'll become moving forward. This trust can be shaken by the questioning that's a part of normal life development.

There may be people within your life that you've always trusted and continue to trust without question. Others you may no longer trust but still accept as a part of your life.

There may be some individuals whom you no longer trust and have decided to cut from your life, because the lack of trust was too uncomfortable to live with.

What has each of these individuals taught you about what trust means to you? How has your definition changed after each experience of losing trust—or has it changed at all?

If a relationship or friendship continues without trust, it can begin to close down communication, empathy, emotions, connection— many of the elements that were necessary for the relationship to develop to begin with.

When trust is lost, it slowly begins to affect every area of your life. Like an earthquake beginning with small tremors that only get bigger, loss of trust begins to undermine the happy memories you've built over the years.

Being able to love someone and being able to trust someone are inextricably linked in many people's minds; however, these two aspects of a relationship are actually very different.

The trust between two people may be broken, but this doesn't mean the love isn't still present, which can make the process of letting someone go even more difficult and confusing. When trust breaks, you may try to hold on to the memory of trust that was present in the relationship in the past to balance out the love for the individual who's still very much present and for whom you have deep feelings.

Trust can be difficult to rebuild and restore, because it can never be the same as it once was; therefore, it can be easier to hold on to a time in the past when there was little or no doubt of the person's trustworthiness.

Once you begin to see these cracks in your sense of trust for what they truly are—within yourself and within your relationship— you always have a choice.

You can choose to try to repair them to keep everything you've known afloat and ignore that the foundation isn't what it used to be. This could result in the walls caving in—hurting you, the person you've lost trust with, and maybe even others around you.

The other option is to embrace the reality and accept the sometimes-painful emotions you're feeling and the actions that need to be taken when you realize you're not able to trust the person the way you once did.

It's not about blaming yourself or another; it's simply expressing to yourself the reality of what you're truly seeing, what you're feeling, and what you know is right and true for you.

Sometimes, you have to let the walls cave in. Like everything in life, all relationships naturally change; every situation is different, and life keeps evolving. The only one who can make the decision about whether to move on is you.

Even if you want to, you won't always have the option to rebuild your relationship to be exactly the same as it once was. If you have the genuine desire to do this, you might be able to build something new where those foundations once stood.

If you've learned from the past, building new foundations can be an experience worth having. As long as you're honest with yourself and with the person in whom you've lost trust, you'll know whether you want to try to build another foundation with that person—or not.

Let's Take a Little Moment

Questions to Reflect Upon

1. What does trust mean to you?
2. Who do you trust the most at this time in your life?
3. Do you find it difficult to trust yourself?
4. Think of a time in your life when your trust was broken. How did this impact you?
5. Who are the people in your life who trust you the most?
6. How important do you feel trust is in your friendships and relationships?
7. Do you find it easy to trust others? What are the foundations you need for there to be trust?

A Reminder to Myself

- ♡ I recognize that there are people in my life whom I trust and, for that, I'm grateful.
- ♡ Trusting others might make me feel uncomfortable at times, but I recognize that it's important to my ongoing growth.
- ♡ By trusting myself, I'm opening myself up to trust others.
- ♡ I allow myself to take my time in building my trust in others.
- ♡ I understand and accept that I may trust different people in different ways.
- ♡ The more I learn about myself, the more I trust where life is taking me.

"When you make a decision because it feels right—not because of how it looks to others—you know it's the right thing to do."

Gareth Michael

18

Frustration

"Frustration—the feeling of being upset or annoyed as a result of being unable to change or achieve something."
- Oxford Dictionary

I t probably goes without saying that you've felt frustrated many times in your life. You've experienced this emotion since you were born, but it was years before you were old enough to have a logical understanding or definition of it. Recognizing it can be helpful, but frustration will likely remain one of the most persistent emotions in your life.

There are many reasons why frustration arises. Some of the most common causes include:

- when you feel people don't understand you;
- when you feel your voice isn't being heard;
- when it seems your concerns or emotions aren't taken seriously; and
- when you're not given the chance to express who you truly are or who you dream you could be.

Frustration is a feeling that often arises due to stress you've put on yourself or pressure that may have been building due to external factors—family, friends, career, or finances. You can have frustration when you don't achieve a goal or from the pressure of trying to achieve that goal—even if you're successful.

Some people may criticize you for being too human in a world where you're expected to perform like a machine, while others may criticize you for being too much like a machine. It seems you can't win, and that's always frustrating.

Before exploring the role of frustration in your life, it's important to ask yourself the question: "How much do I truly understand myself?"

This question itself may bring up frustration, but it's essential to investigate what causes you to feel frustration so you can begin to address it.

You may feel you've spent a lifetime trying to understand who you are, but, every time you get comfortable with who you believe you are, some situation or change happens that makes you question yourself once again. Even when you can see growth as a result of the experience, that doesn't mean the process wasn't frustrating at times—and that's okay.

In this stress-filled world, frustration is often just below the surface.

Consider your sense of purpose in life. You may feel frustrated about your perceived lack of purpose, or you may understand your purpose but feel frustrated at your lack of clarity about how to achieve it.

You may feel frustrated that nobody can tell you what that purpose is or frustrated when you feel you're just starting to feel some confidence about what it is, and then it seems to change again.

Such constant changes—which are the rule in life, not the exception—can be especially frustrating.

Many times, people don't express how difficult or painful changes are. They bury their emotions in an effort to not feel the pain in the experience, such as in a break-up or loss of a job. By not expressing how they feel, they suffer more.

Living with constant frustration can turn to anger—which is a very different emotion. Sometimes it's difficult to show frustration, because people perceive it as anger. This causes more frustration, which can turn to anger.

Frustration is actually a healthy emotion, as it anchors you in reality. If you never feel frustration, you're not living in reality—you're likely only allowing yourself to feel certain emotions or hiding from recognizing the truth about yourself or a situation.

Living with emotions can be frustrating, but it would definitely be much more frustrating trying to live a life without them.

There's no need to fear frustration. It won't ruin your life, and it can genuinely help to solve problems. When you feel it, you're seeing the problem for what it is.

Once you express the frustration, you can then relax and work on coming up with an effective solution. However, if you suppress the frustration or allow it to build up and explode into anger, you won't get past it.

Frustration is, in many ways, an especially challenging emotion, because you can become frustrated by other emotions you're feeling. So, you're having a feeling about a feeling!

Remember that frustration is a natural emotion, one that won't likely ever go away. However, you can learn to recognize it for what it is, investigate its source, and, in the process, find insight and strength.

Let's Take a Little Moment

Questions to Reflect Upon

1. What other emotions do you commonly feel when you're frustrated?

2. Can you accept that frustration may always be a part of your life?

3. How do you currently deal with frustration?

4. In what areas of your life are you currently experiencing frustration?

5. What individuals do you regularly find frustrating?

6. In what ways do you frustrate yourself?

7. Do you feel comfortable expressing your frustration? If so, to whom?

8. If everyone experiences frustration, why can it be difficult to talk to others about it?

9. Can you think of a time in your life when frustration prompted you to subsequently take action?

A Reminder to Myself

♡ Frustration is a part of me, but it doesn't define who I am.

♡ I accept challenges as a normal part of life and know that I've always learned from them.

♡ I allow myself to express frustration in the same way I express any of my other emotions.

♡ Living with my emotions can be frustrating, but I know it would definitely be more frustrating to live a life without them.

♡ I recognize that frustration is a natural feeling, and I know that spending time with it will help me to process it and let it go.

"Life tends to present a lot of
challenges, because a large part of your
experience in being here is to grow."

Gareth Michael

19

Labels

"Label—a classifying phrase or name applied to a person or thing, especially one that is inaccurate or restrictive."
- Oxford Dictionary

From the moment you begin to understand words, you learn labels for everything.

Everything you've ever experienced, everything you see around you, and everything you think about has likely been labeled by someone before you, and more things continue to get labeled each and every day.

If it weren't for the labels placed on things, communication among your family, friends, and colleagues would be difficult or possibly non-existent.

Labels can be powerful and bring people together, but they can also divide individuals, communities, and nations.

Before modern technology and travel, the people of each country around the world found their own way to label the things they saw around them, and they used these labels to be able to communicate and share with one another.

Labeling was an essential building block of the 7000+ languages used and taught around the world to this day. Dictionaries and translations of books and documents were created to share these labels with others, enhancing the unity and understanding among all people.

As the beauty that is language developed, words became more and more strictly defined. However, in reality, some things are harder to define than others, and dictionary definitions can sometimes limit and constrain full understanding of certain situations and ideas.

This is especially true for labels that contain judgment such as "good," "bad," "right," "wrong," "normal," etc. Everyone may use the same words, but those words can still mean different things to different people.

Emotions are a prime example of something that can have different meanings for each individual within the same language. Each person feels emotion differently, so even though creating definitions of emotions and breaking them down into categories can be helpful, at times these definitions are taken literally.

This can limit a person to what they've learned is acceptable to feel as opposed to what they truly feel. From a young age, you've been taught by others how to define your feelings. But, in reality, that understanding could be quite restrictive at times and not do justice to your true range of emotions.

From the moment you were born and began to learn your first language, you were taught a multitude of labels—your gender, your first and last name, your nationality, the country you lived in, the color of your hair, your weight, your age. These definitions of yourself that others taught you are all that you and everybody else have known in life.

In addition to these descriptive labels, there are labels that indicate the value or social acceptance of things. Since you've always been taught that things should fit within these labels, it's understandable that, when something or someone challenges your label or your definition of something, it may trigger emotions—for instance, anger, frustration, or annoyance.

When you label something, you may feel a sense of safety and certainty in talking about that subject. In some ways, you may feel you're allowed to participate in the conversation around it.

When someone uses a label differently than you would or begins to question or redefine it—especially if their questions make sense—admitting they might have a point could change the way you view many things.

People aren't always fond of changing how they label things due to the emotion and uncertainty this stirs up. It can be scary to explore the true meaning of what you're feeling or even to begin to question it.

Just as with definitions of other things, this exploration can open a door to a lot more questions about the truth of your emotions and how you've labeled things throughout your life.
Uncertainty about these parts of yourself can be stressful, but it can also bring rewarding growth.

Many people operate from the idea there must always be someone who's right and someone who's wrong. There must be a strict definition of what something means with no room for grey areas or different perspectives.

Yet, those 7,000+ languages impact people in different but equal ways, allowing them to communicate and understand the world around them. So, is it really reasonable for someone to decide that the way they label something is correct and everyone else is wrong?

As you move through life, you don't have to hold on to the same strict definitions you were taught by others. You can allow yourself to ask questions, arrive at your own definitions, and understand why someone has labeled something differently than you have.

Remember, there are 7,000+ ways to say the same thing on this Earth—and they're all correct.

Embrace the growth that comes from trying to understand a perspective that's different from your own. If you're open to understanding how other people have defined something, you could learn a lot about yourself, others, and the world.

Let's Take a Little Moment

Questions to Reflect Upon

1. When looking at yourself in the mirror, what labels do you use?

2. What labels do you use in your life that you struggle with or find limiting?

3. What emotions have been labeled as acceptable for you to feel?

4. Are there labels in your life you've felt or currently feel protective of? Why?

5. How have the labels you use in your life changed over time?

6. Can you think of times in your life when you felt like others labeled you?

7. Have you ever unintentionally forced your labels onto somebody else?

8. How do you feel when someone doesn't agree with the labels you use?

A Reminder to Myself

♡ I can't change how others use labels, but I can explore and accept what they mean to me.

♡ I look forward to understanding myself, which will assist me in understanding, connecting with, and helping others.

♡ I recognize that if it wasn't for labels, I wouldn't be able to communicate with others.

♡ I know that labels will always be a part of my life, and I'm willing to explore how I feel about them.

♡ By exploring my own use of labels, I'll better understand what they mean to me.

"True power isn't turning others into a version of you but assisting them to be the best version of themselves."

Gareth Michael

20

The Strength of Vulnerability

*It's within your vulnerability that
you find who you truly are.*

Vulnerability can be one of the hardest things to allow yourself to see—never mind showing it to the world. But, at times, this is what the world needs the most.

It's when you accept the vulnerability within yourself that the world sees and accepts it, too.

It may seem surprising, but vulnerability demonstrates an individual's greatest strengths, not their weaknesses. It's a place few are willing to go, but it's where you can learn the most.

It's only when you're willing to be vulnerable that you come to see the true depth and complexity of your own emotions. Truly seeing this allows you to appreciate the journey it's taken to get you to where you are today.

With this realization, you find you're much less likely to judge yourself or others. You become strong by understanding that vulnerability is a key part of your growth. By allowing yourself to be vulnerable, you're able to experience every emotion and scenario within life itself without labeling it.

Vulnerability isn't a place you can be forced into or out of. It's a place in which you find yourself when you least expect it. Many find themselves in this place at multiple times throughout their lives. That doesn't make it any easier to be in it, however. It takes time to process the idea of vulnerability and to understand it.

Vulnerability arises in many forms:

Not knowing how to love yourself, you feel vulnerable. That's okay, but it doesn't mean it's easy.

Not knowing what step to take next, you feel vulnerable. That's okay, but it doesn't mean it's easy.

Feeling lost and not knowing who to trust or love, you feel vulnerable. That's okay, but it doesn't mean it's easy.

Losing a loved one, wanting to communicate or express your emotions but being unable to, you feel vulnerable. That's okay, but it doesn't mean it's easy.

It's okay to sit with yourself and say, "I don't know," especially in a world where you're expected to know everything.

When you become vulnerable in your own company, you truly meet yourself. When two become vulnerable together, each individual truly meets the other.

Nobody can convince you to explore that vulnerable space. You embark on the journey when you sense it's time to do so. When you become comfortable with being vulnerable to yourself and to everyone you meet in this world, you realize it's not one person's particular purpose to convince others that they should be vulnerable, too. You can't explain to anyone else the strength that you find there.

The path to recognizing the strength in vulnerability requires courage and insight. You become an example to the world simply in your ability to accept and process your own emotions and those of others. The wisdom you've gained on your journey is displayed through your manner and your words. This can't be faked.

Simply start by accepting your own vulnerability. The strength you find in that place will change you and inspire others.

Let's Take a Little Moment

Questions to Reflect Upon

1. What does vulnerability mean to you? How do you feel about it?

2. Are you comfortable being vulnerable with others?

3. How do you react when others are being vulnerable with you?

4. If you were to accept your vulnerability, do you fear you'd be seen as weak?

5. Who have you been vulnerable with? What made this person different than others?

6. When you're vulnerable, what other emotions do you feel?

A Reminder to Myself

♡ I know there's strength, not weakness, in understanding my vulnerability.

♡ Accepting that I'm vulnerable helps me to develop my self-confidence and to recognize the inner strength I always knew I had.

♡ I'm open and receptive to experiencing new situations, people, and activities, even when they make me feel vulnerable.

♡ I believe in my inner strength enough to know that I'm going to be okay.

♡ Vulnerability is a part of who I am and, therefore, I look forward to spending time with it.

"You may not be able to control the emotions you experience in life, but building a relationship with them will always help you to learn and grow."

Gareth Michael

If you enjoyed this book,
please consider reviewing it on the Amazon bookstore.
Your time and assistance are much appreciated!

If you'd like to follow Gareth Michael,
you can find him on:

Facebook: @gmwritings
Instagram: @gmwritings

Visit www.garethmichael.com
to read more about the author.

We value your feedback and input. If you have any
thoughts you'd like to share or requests for new content,
please email us at hello@garethmichael.com

About the Author

Gareth Michael delivers inspirational support and guidance to tens of thousands of people across the globe.

From a young age, Gareth experienced personal and family challenges including depression, an unforeseen family death, cancer, and bankruptcy.

Growing up through this, Gareth learned the true value of expression and found he had an intuitive gift for helping others.

This gift has been channeled into a host of international events across eight countries on four continents, creating an incredibly supportive online following.

Gareth Michael completed *Ever-changing Perspectives* at the age of 20 and released it at the age of 21. It's his first published book.

Printed in Great Britain
by Amazon